Grandeur *in the* Republic of Georgia

FROM SIGNAGI TO STEPANTSMINDA

A TRAVEL PHOTO ART BOOK

LAINE CUNNINGHAM

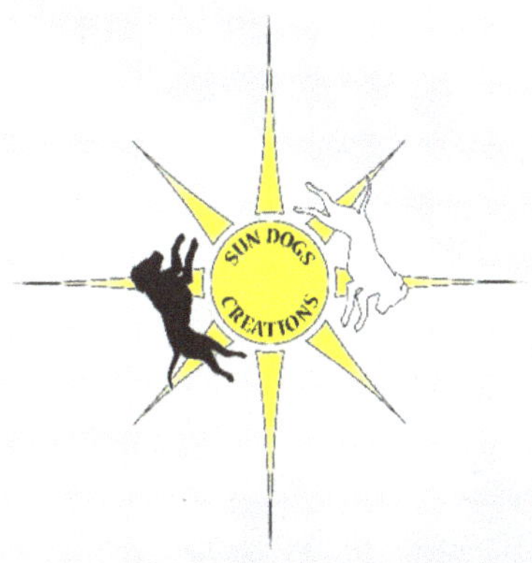

Grandeur in the Republic of Georgia

From Signagi to Stepantsminda

A Travel Photo Art Book

Published by Sun Dogs Creations
Changing the World One Book at a Time
Print ISBN: 9781946732873

Cover Design by Angel Leya

THE TRAVEL PHOTO ART SERIES

Bikes of Berlin

Necropolises of New Orleans I & II

Ruins of Rome I & II

Ancients of Assisi I & II

Panoramas of Portugal

Nuances of New York

Glimpses of Germany

Impressions of Italy

Altitudes of the Alps

Knights Through the Ages

Coast of California

Utopia of the Unicorn

Flourishes of France

Portraits of Paris

Tableaus of Tbilisi

GLIDE

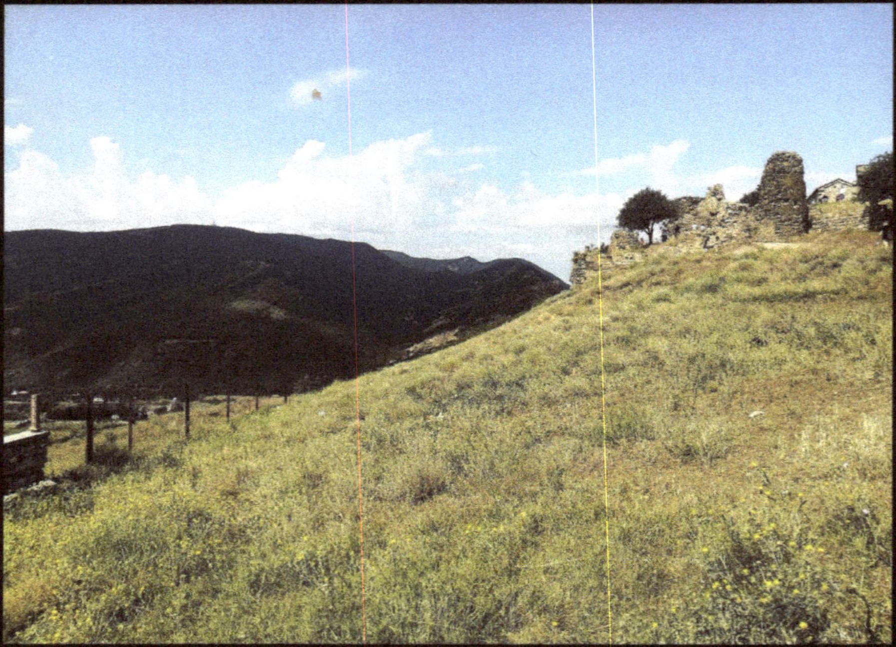

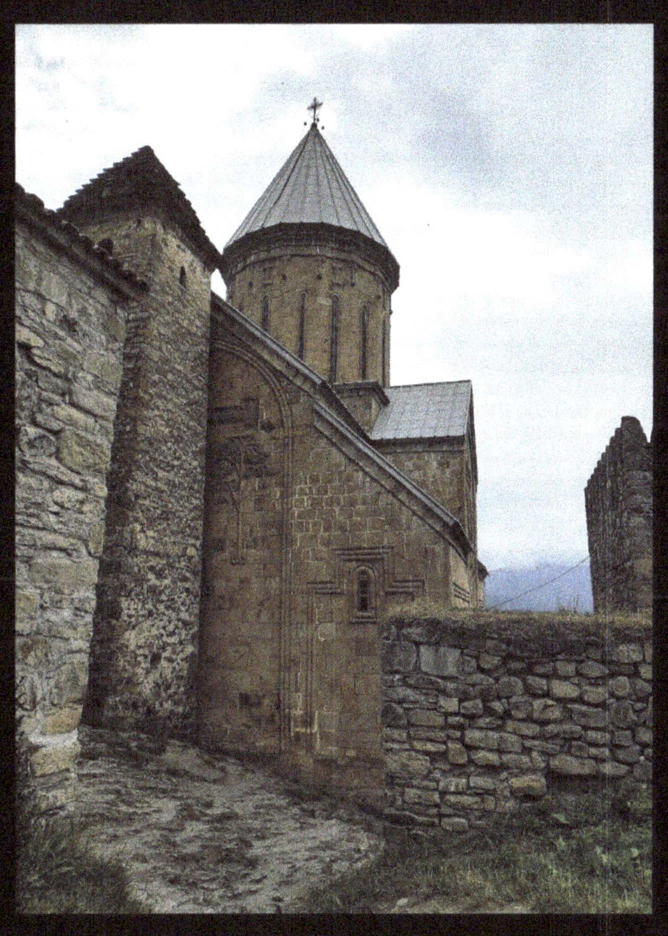

COLLAGE

MESSAGES

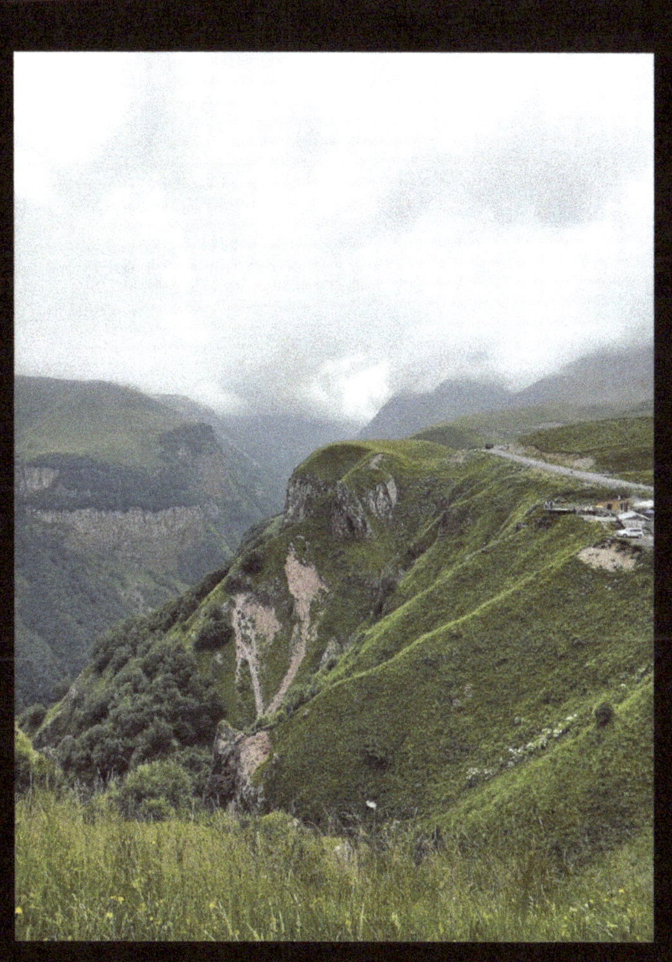

POLLOCKESQUE

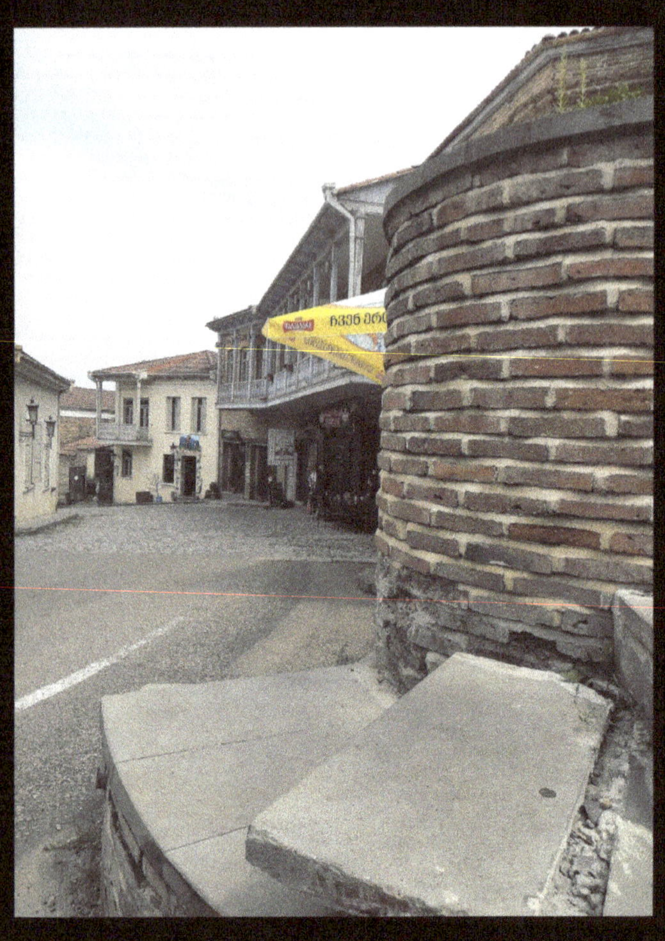

PASTRY

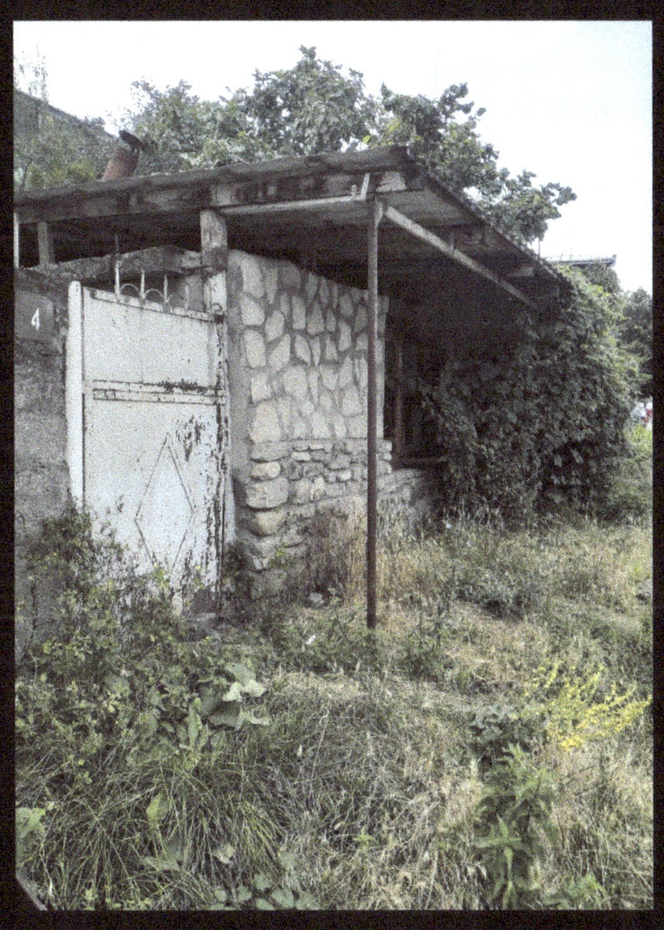

4 MAIN STREET

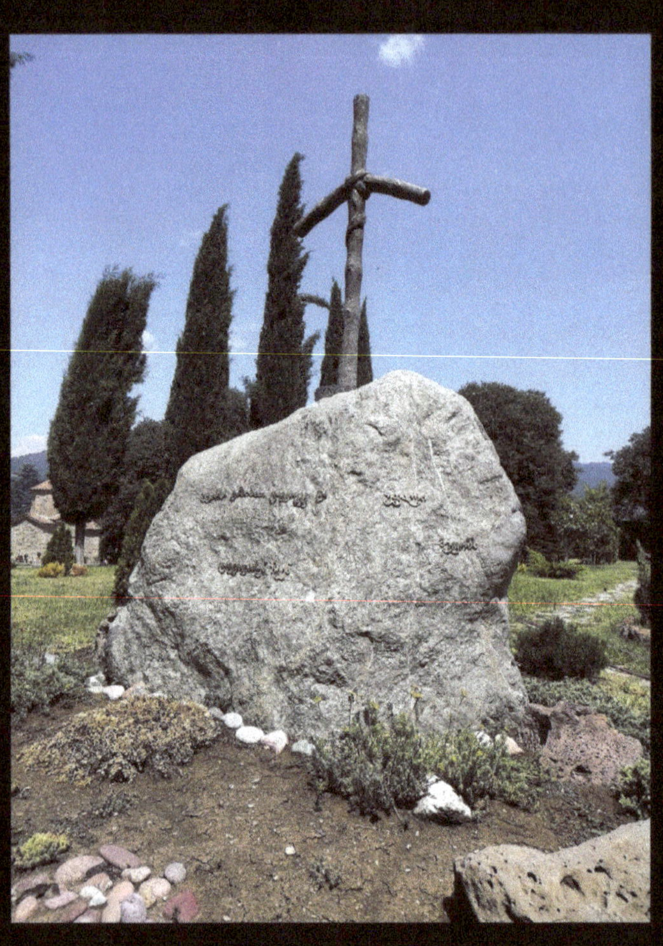

ARTHURIAN

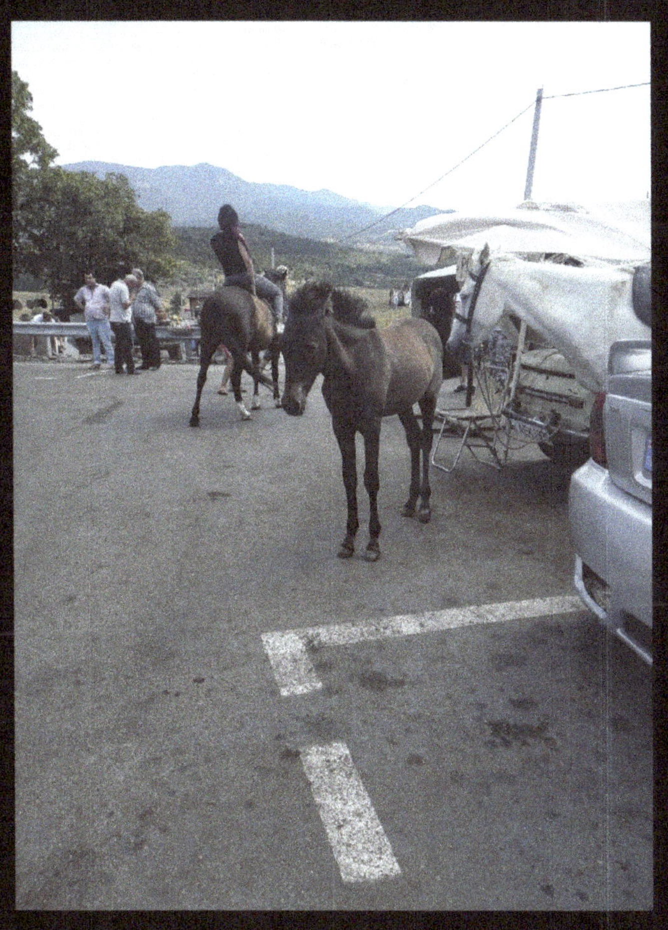

FRIENDSHIP

YOUTH

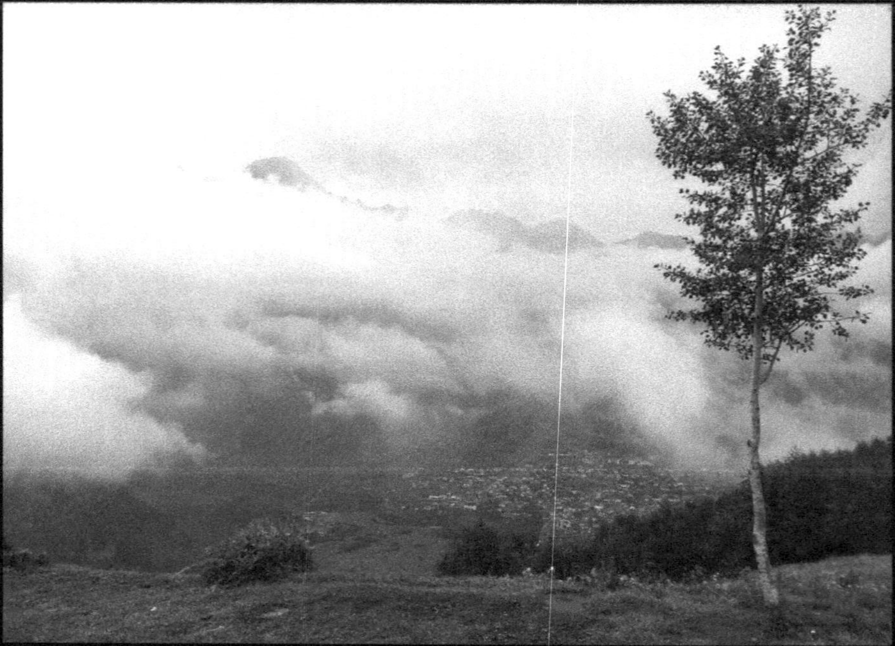

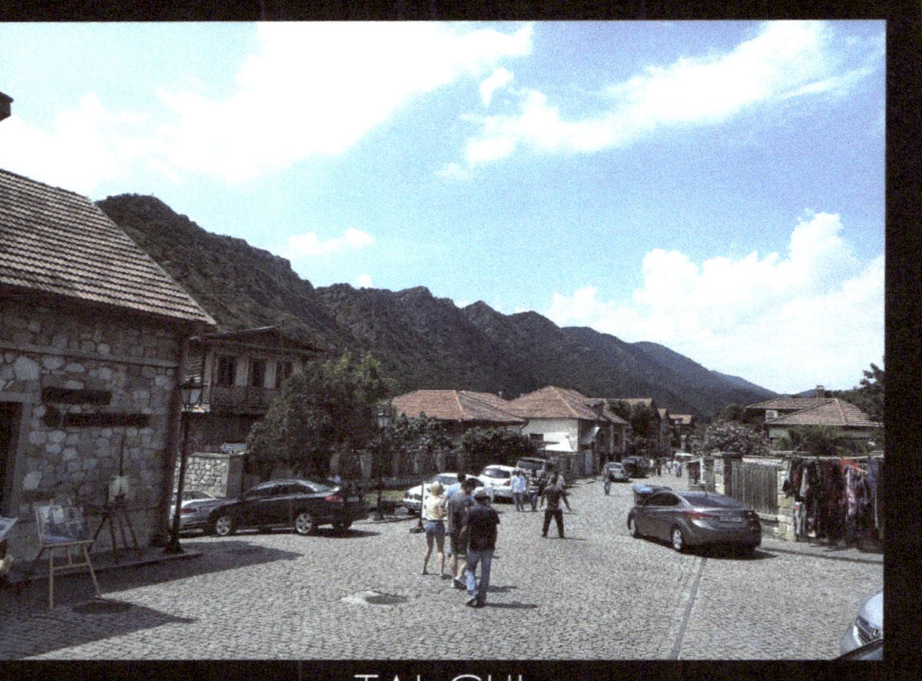
TAI CHI

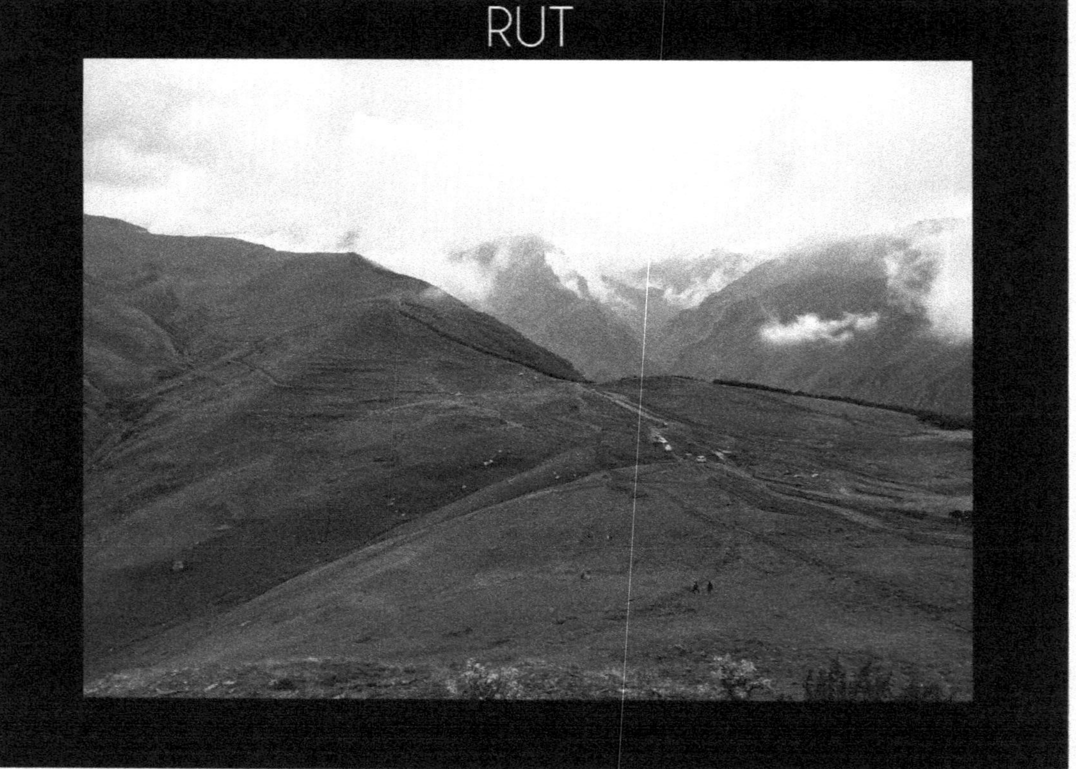
RUT

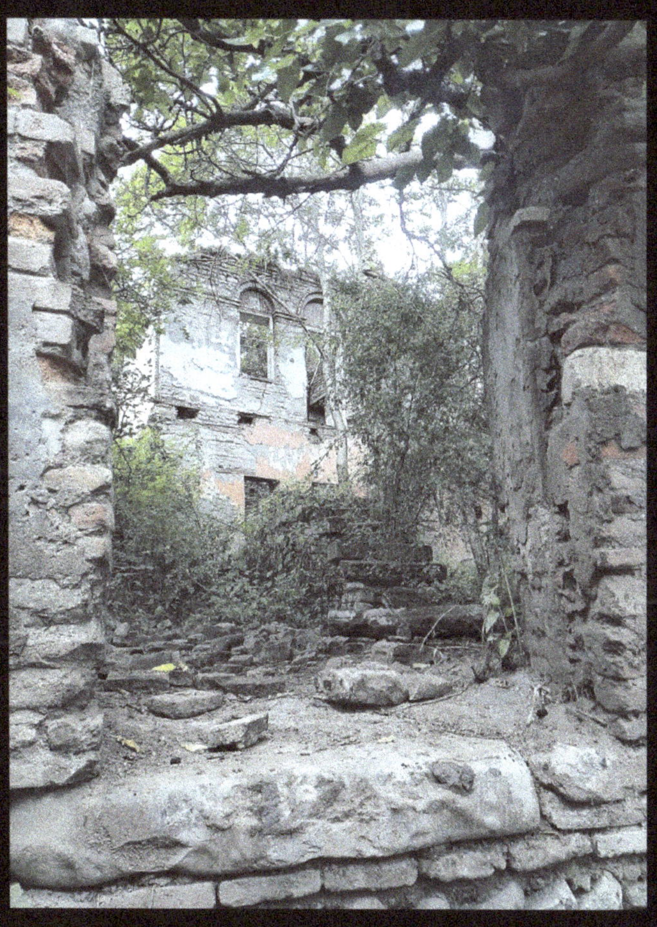

SKIN DEEP

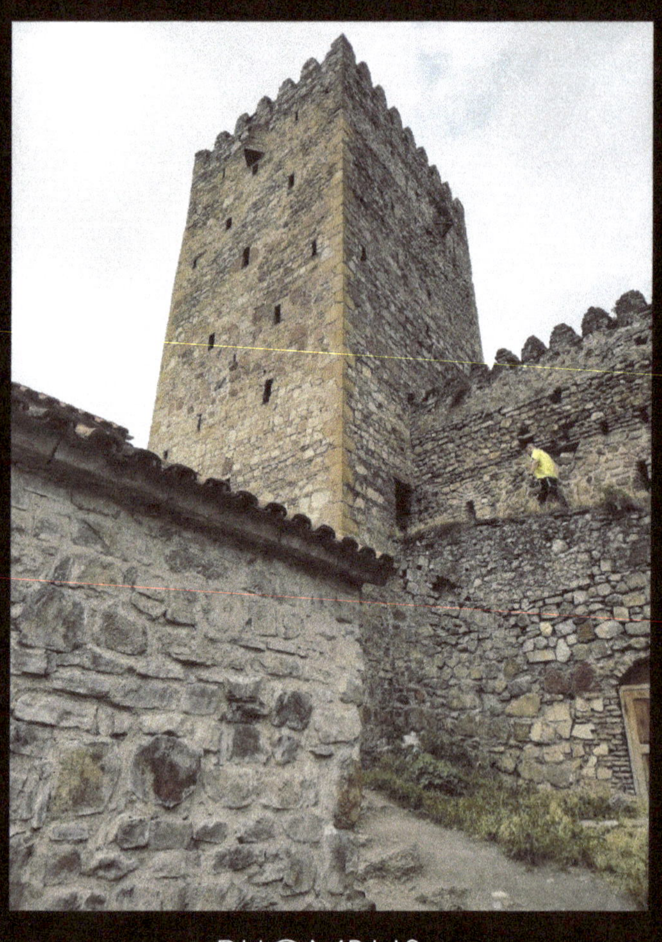

RHOMBUS

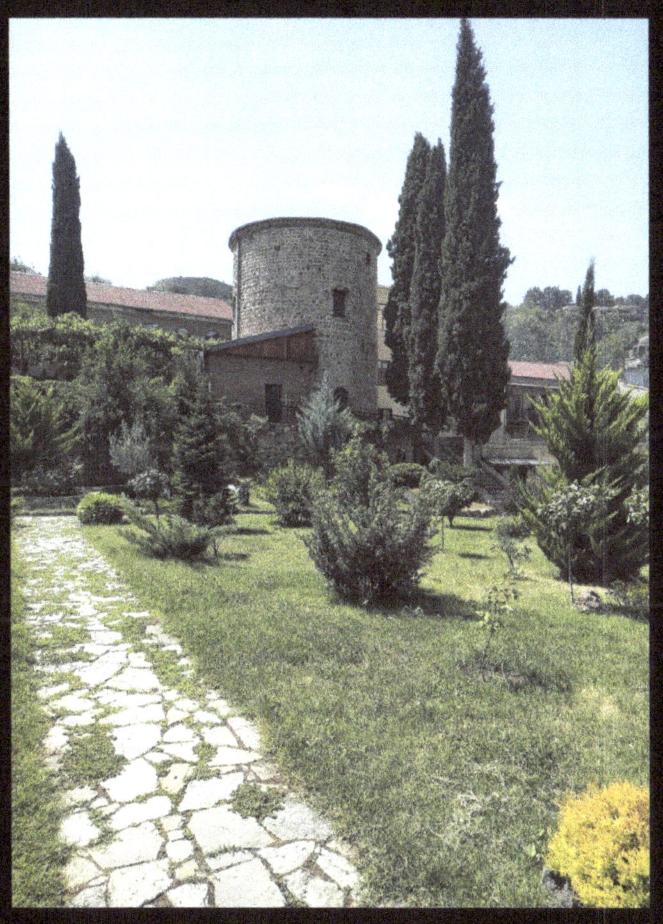

EVERGREEN

BYWAYS

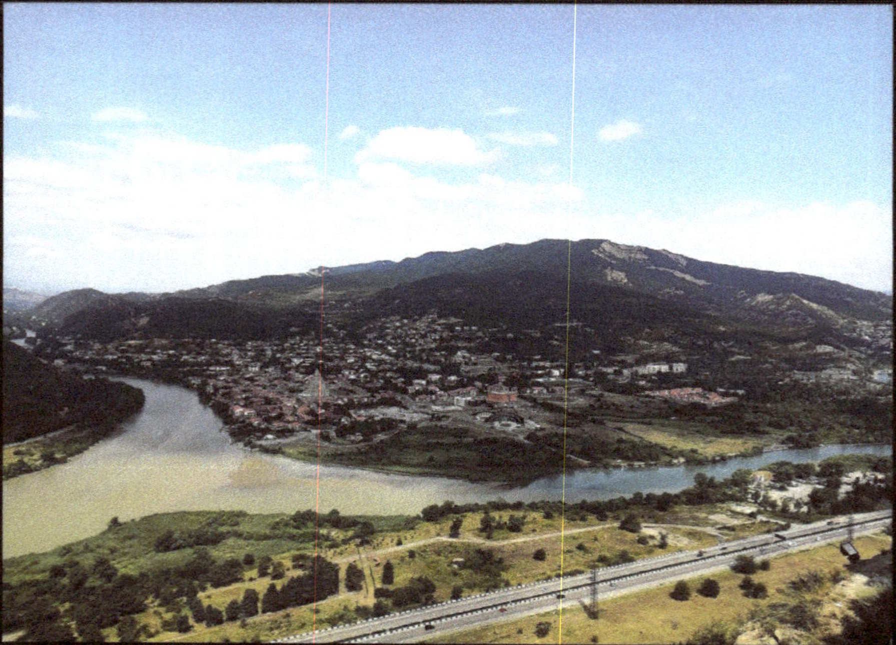

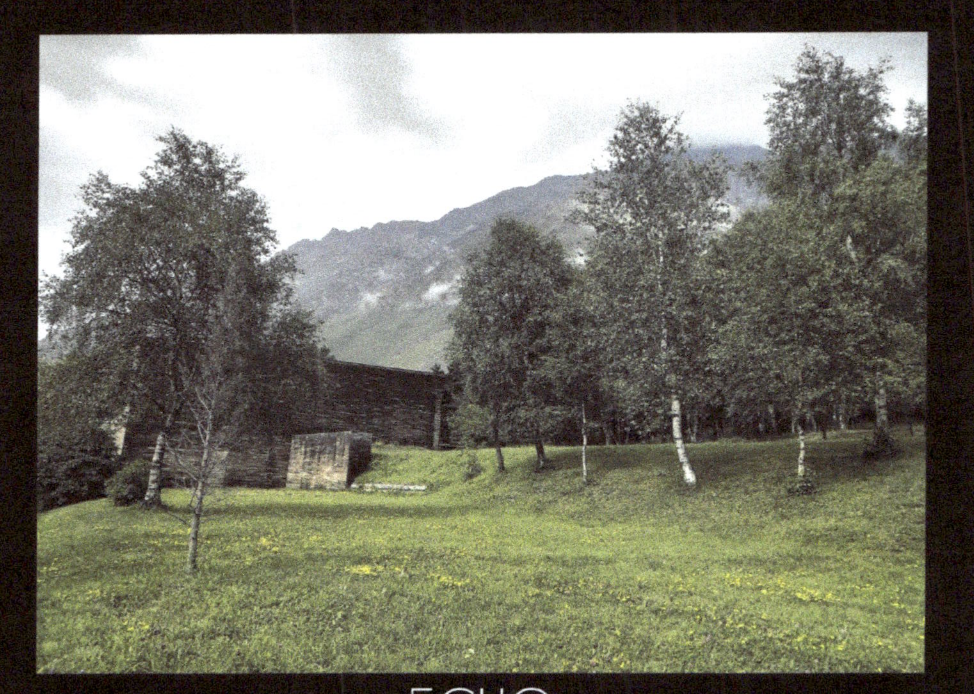

ECHO

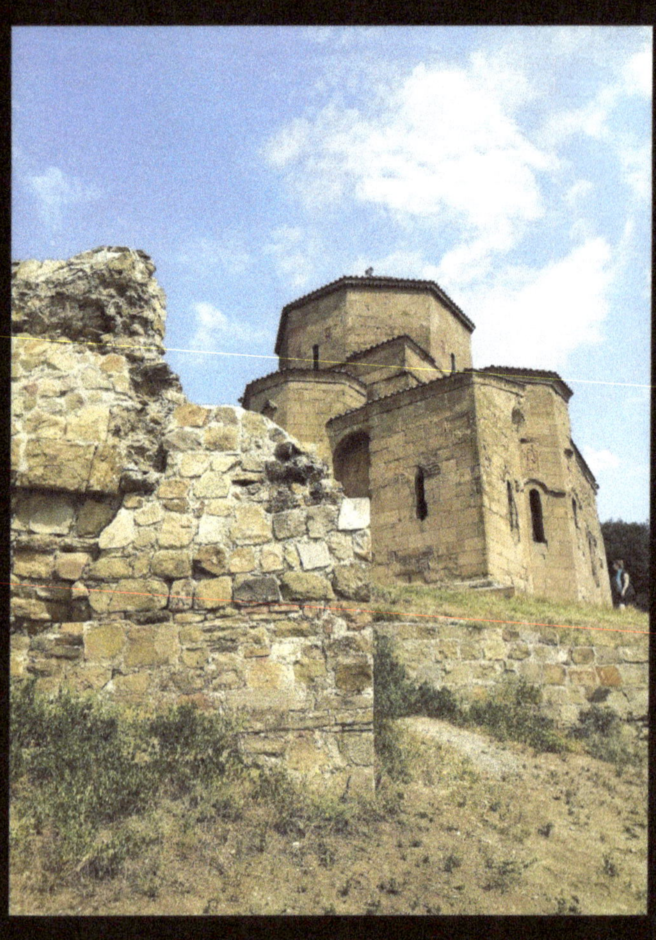

JIGSAW

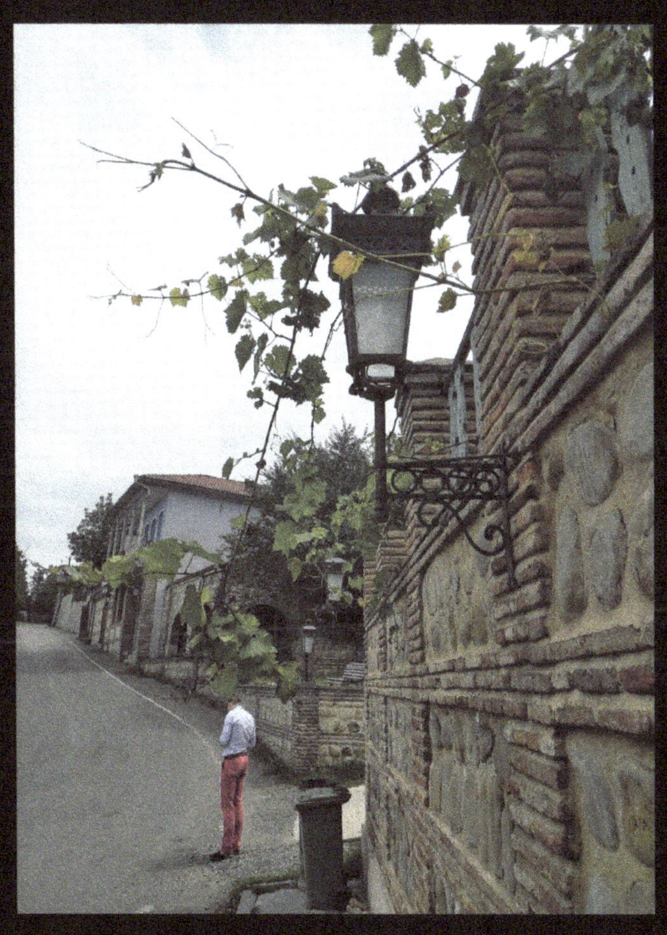

LOOP THE LOOP

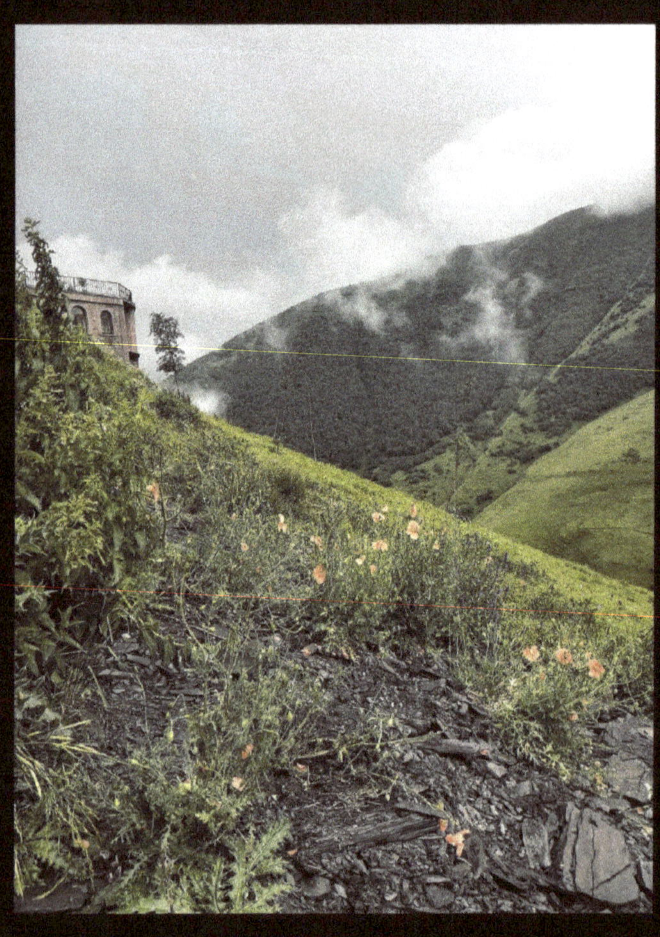

CRISSCROSS

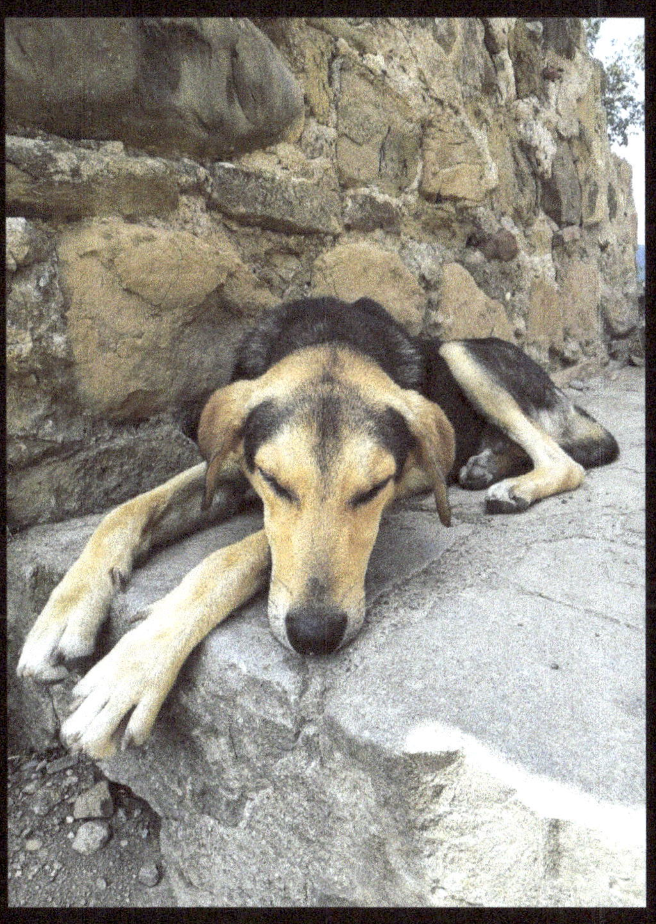

CONTENTMENT

NATURAL HEART

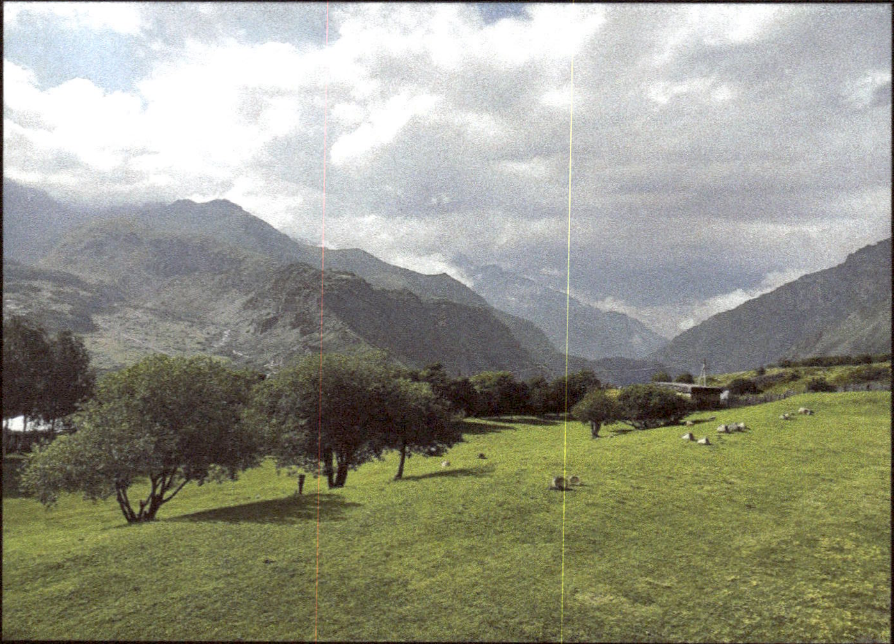

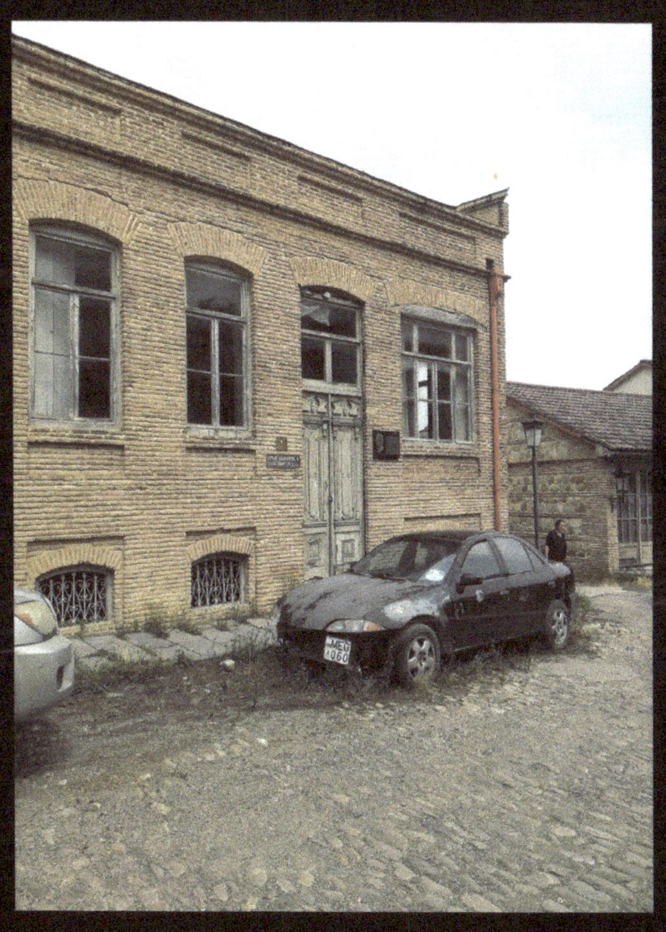

MODERN RELIC

REPLAY

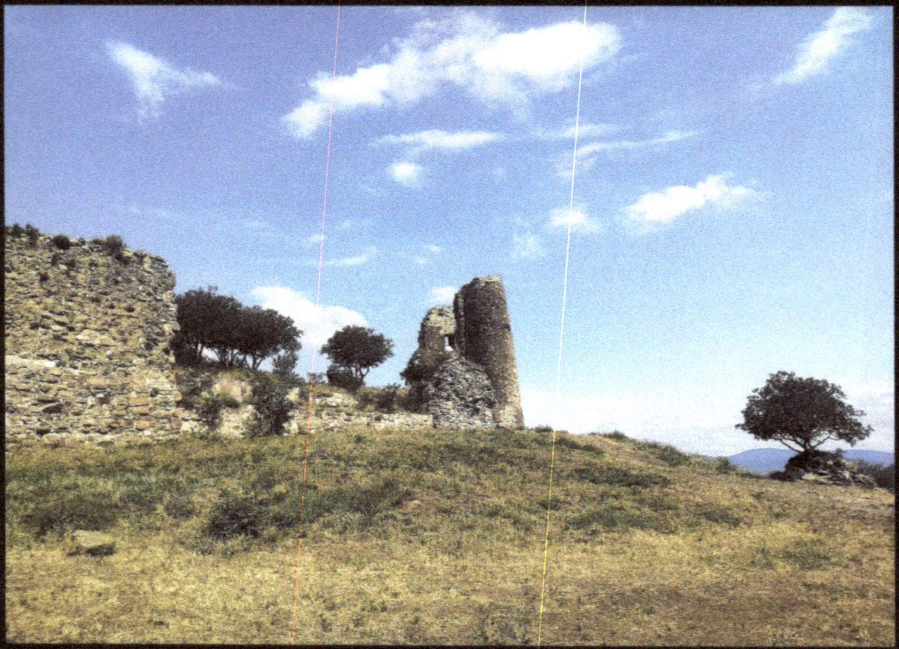

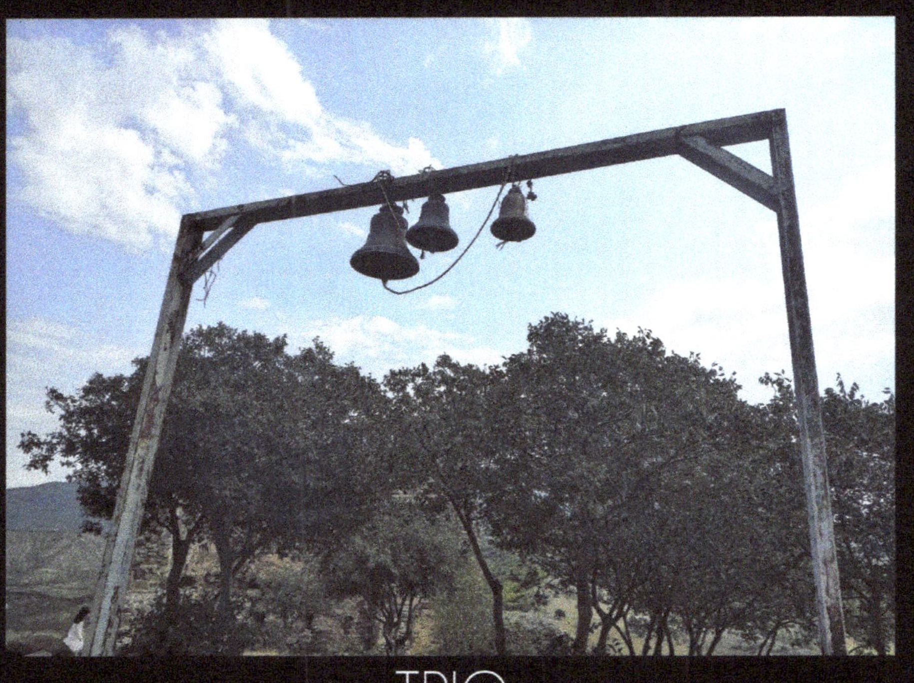

TRIO

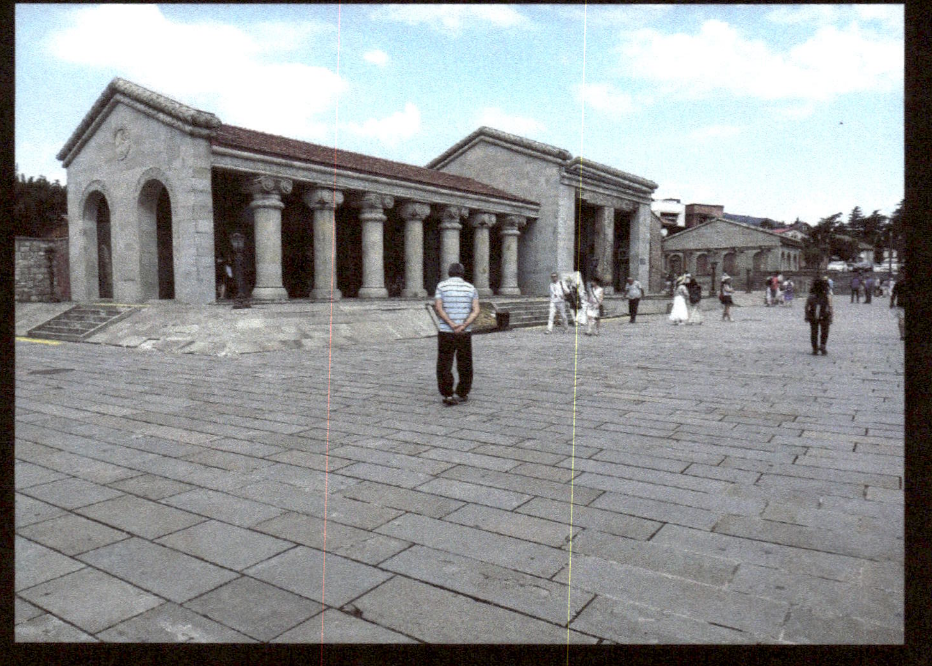
STAGE SET

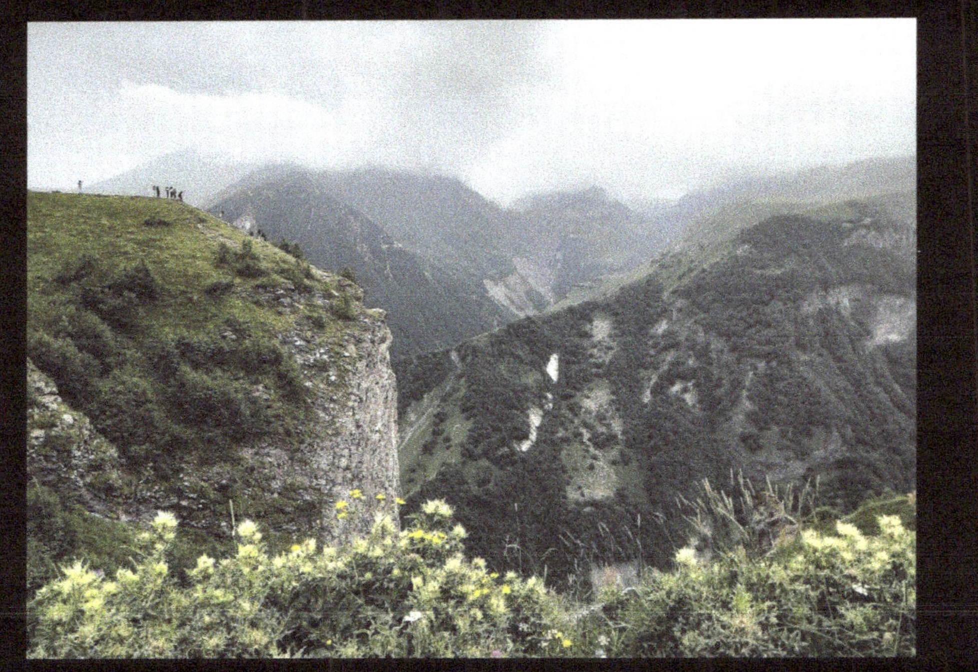
BILLY GOATS

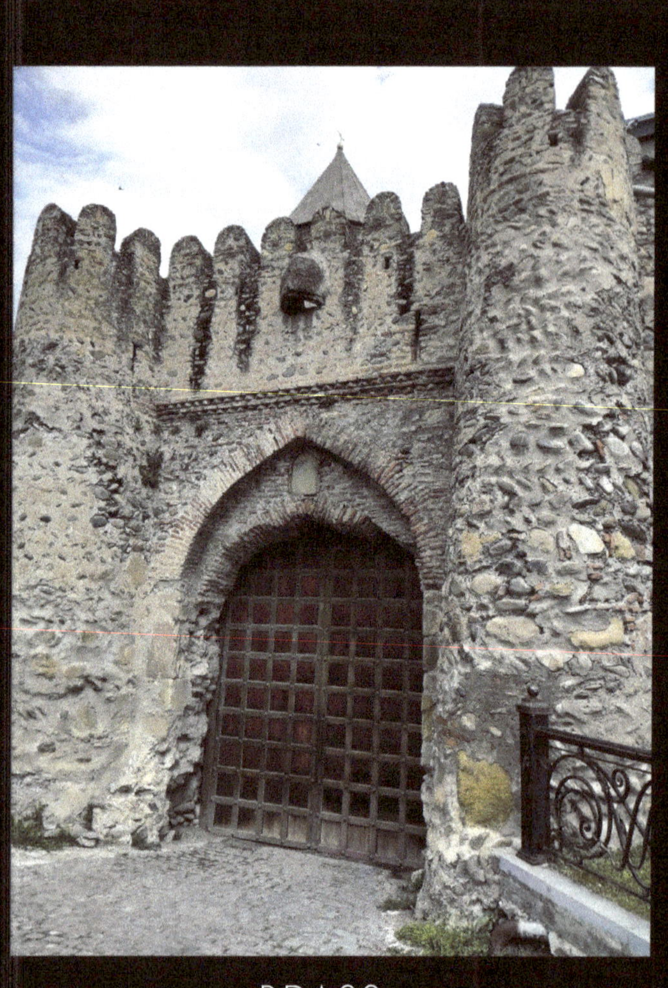

BRASS

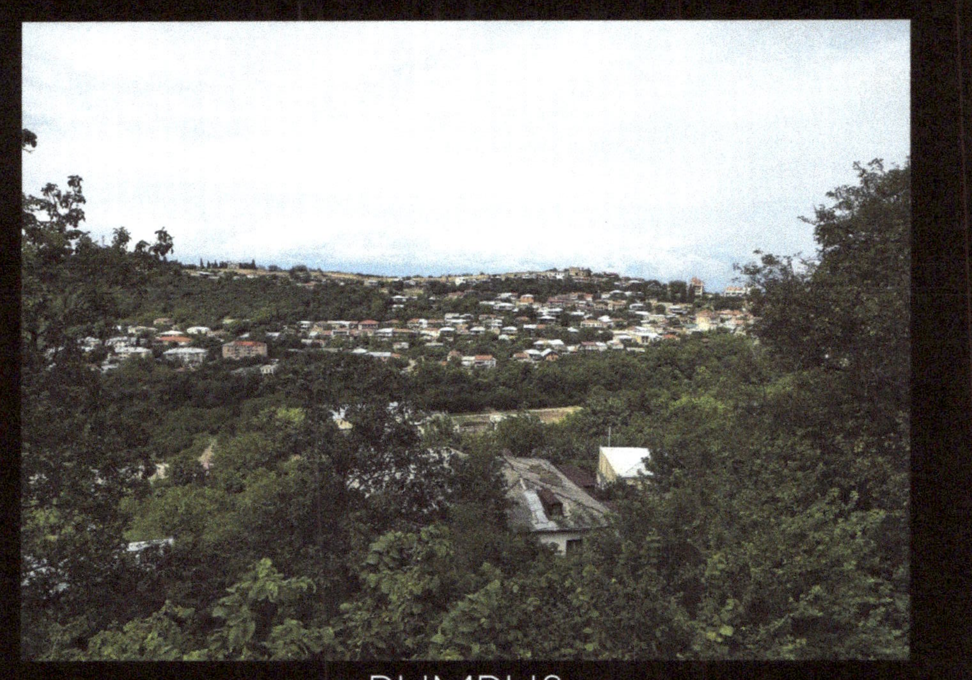
RUMPUS

SLEEPING GIANT

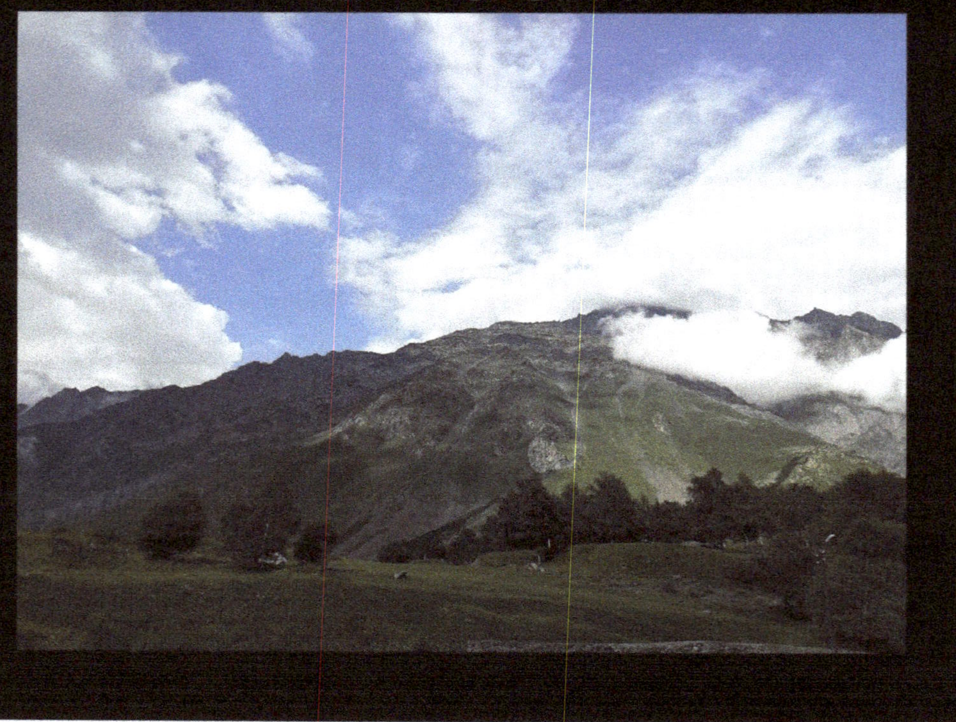

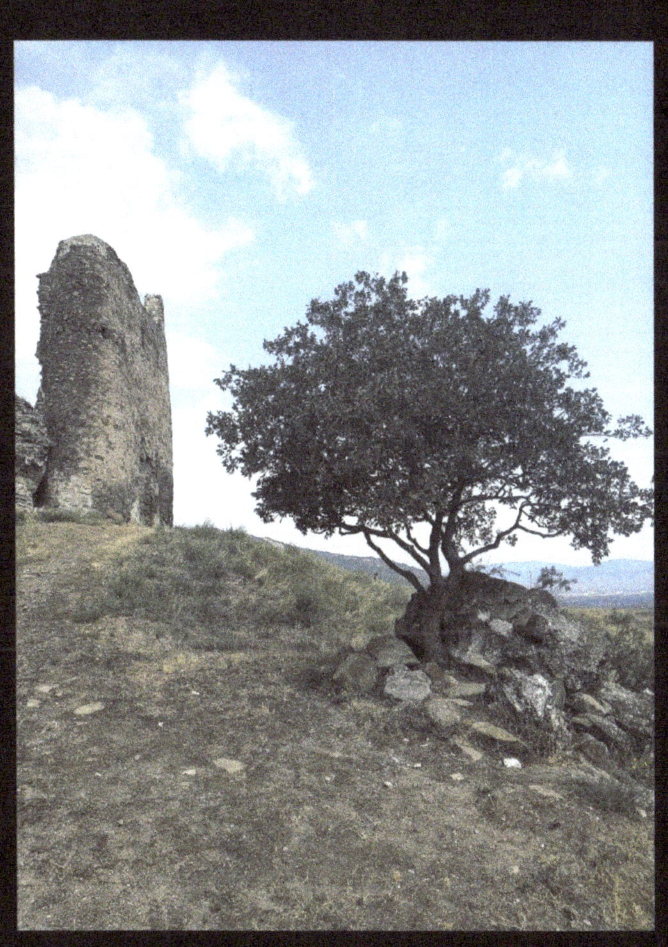

OUTBACK

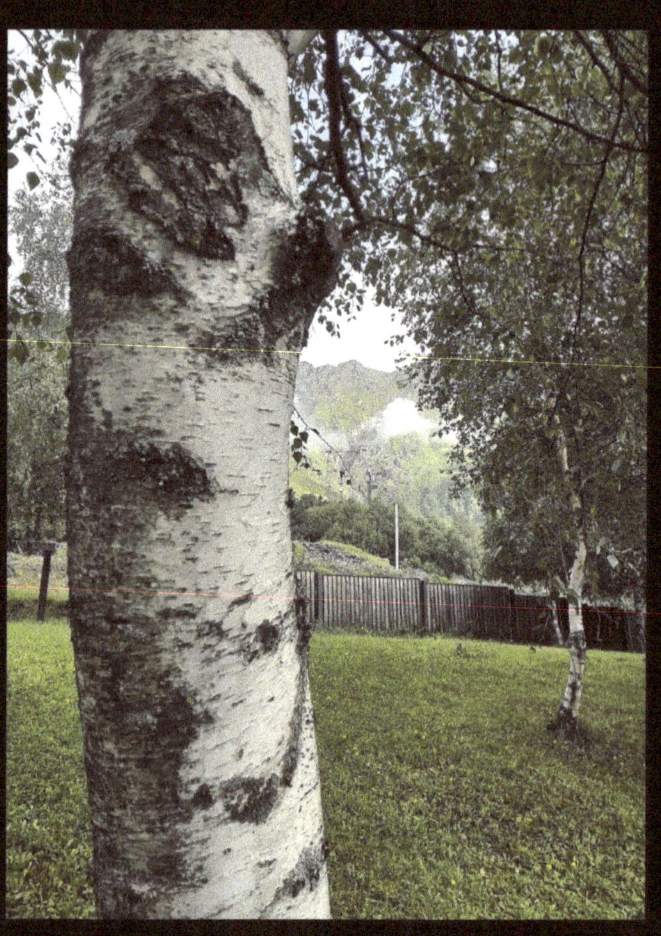

BETWEEN, BEYOND

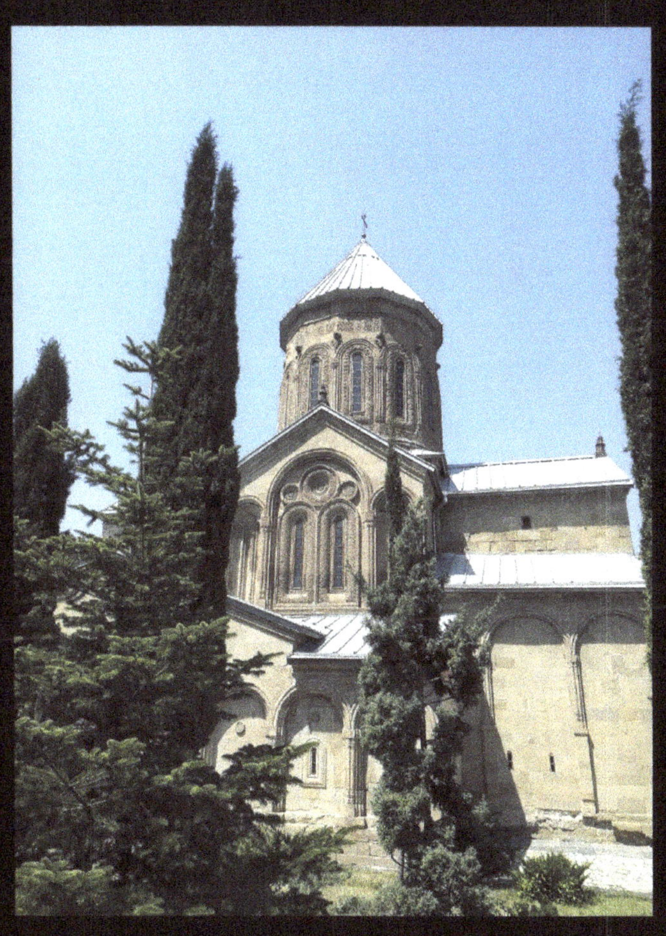
CONES AND PLANES

BRIDAL

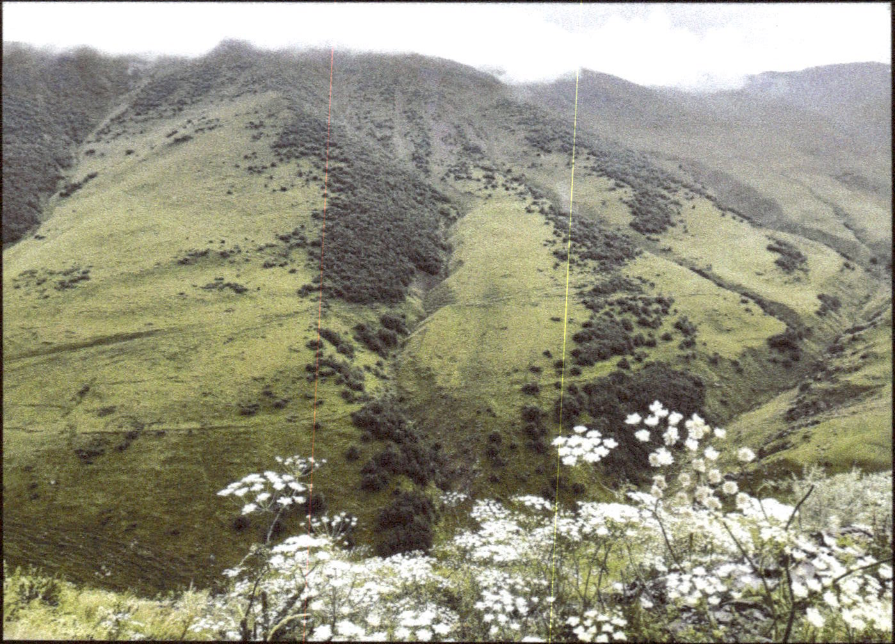

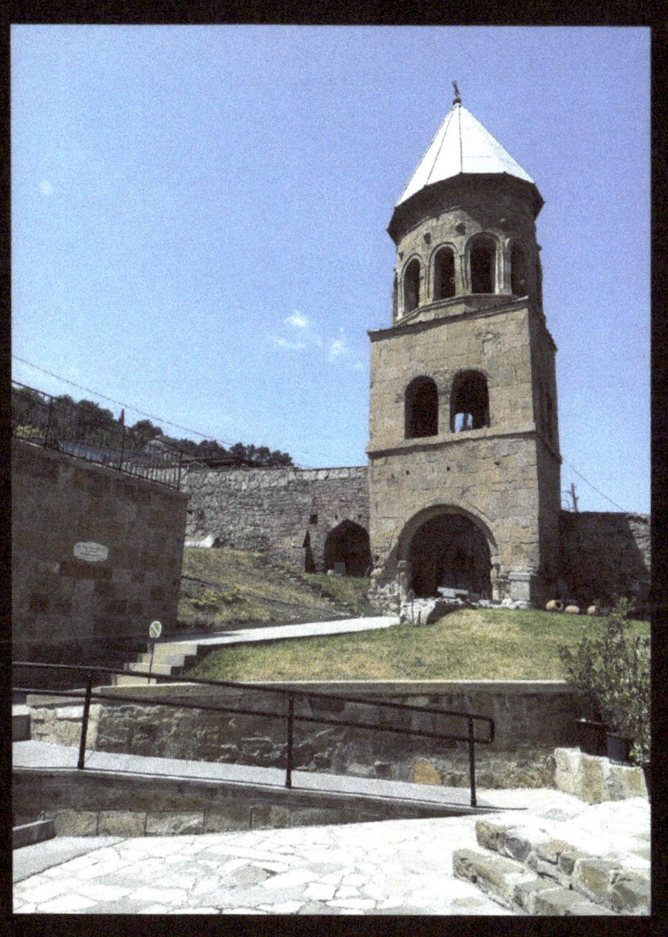

CRAYON

BARRIERS

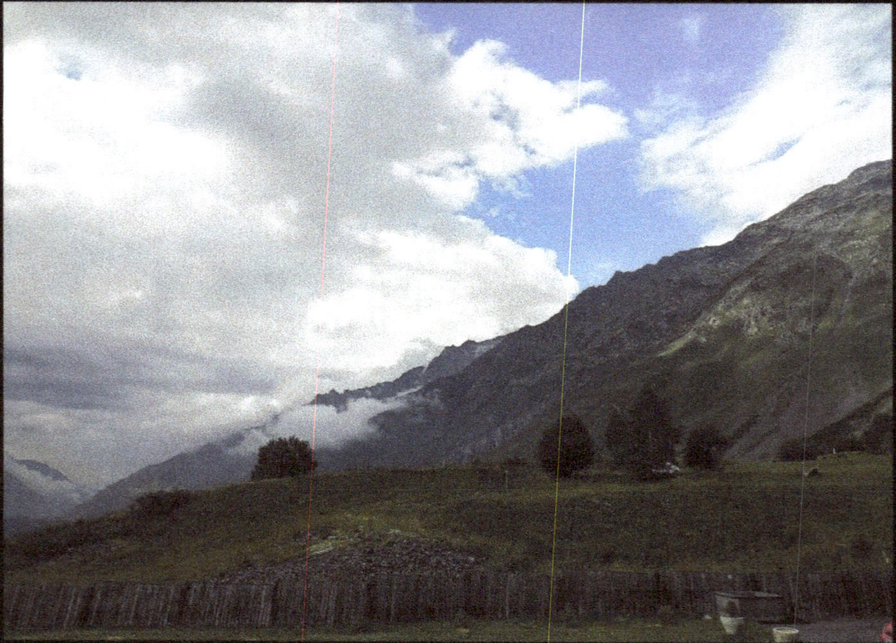

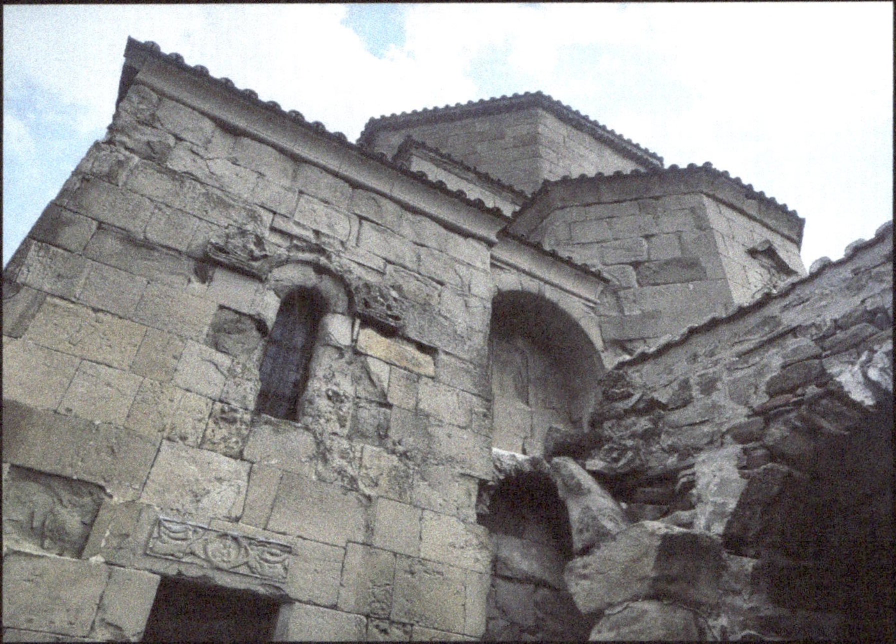

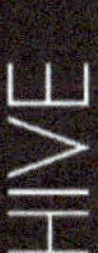

SPREAD

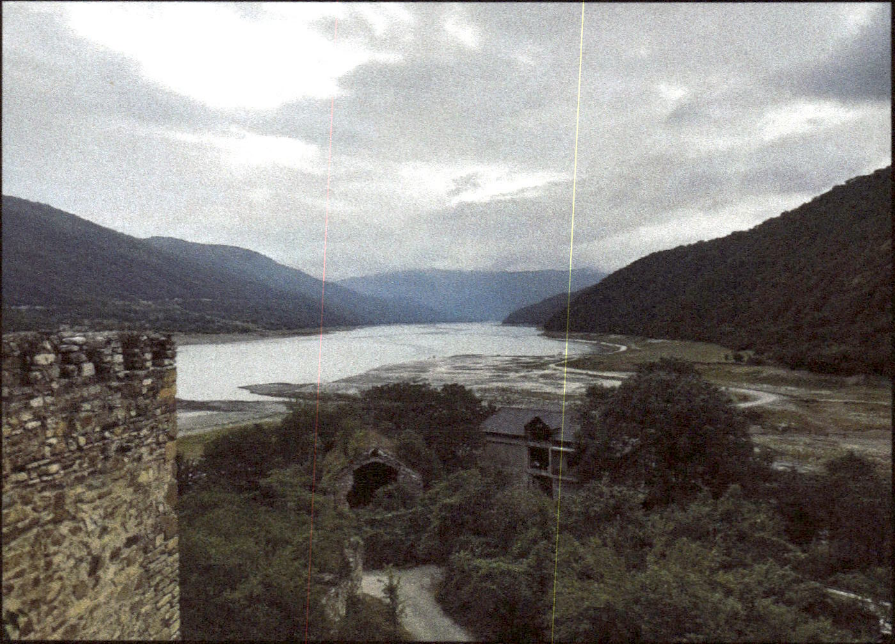

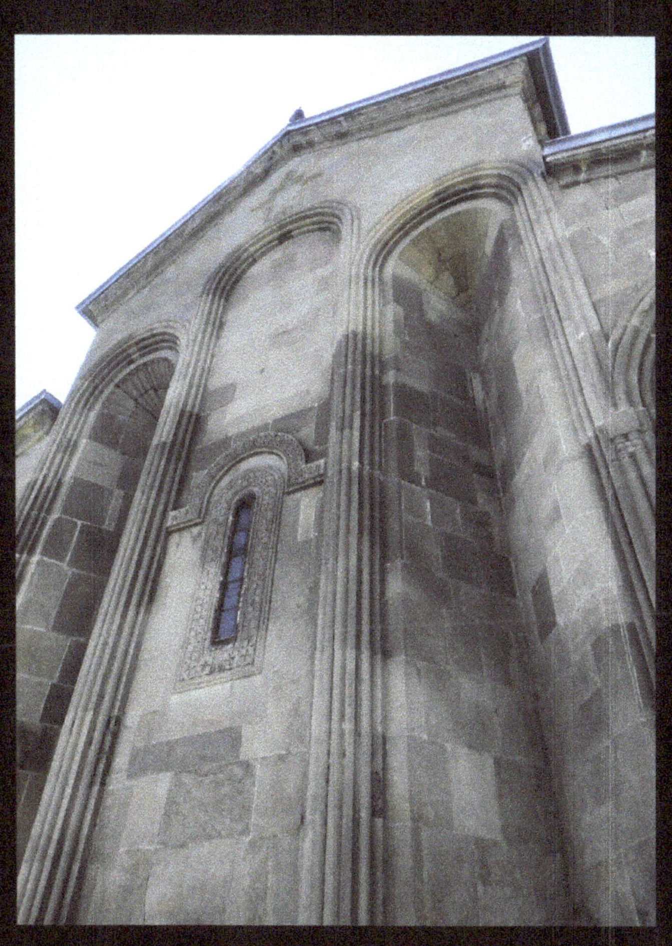
ANGEL LIGHT

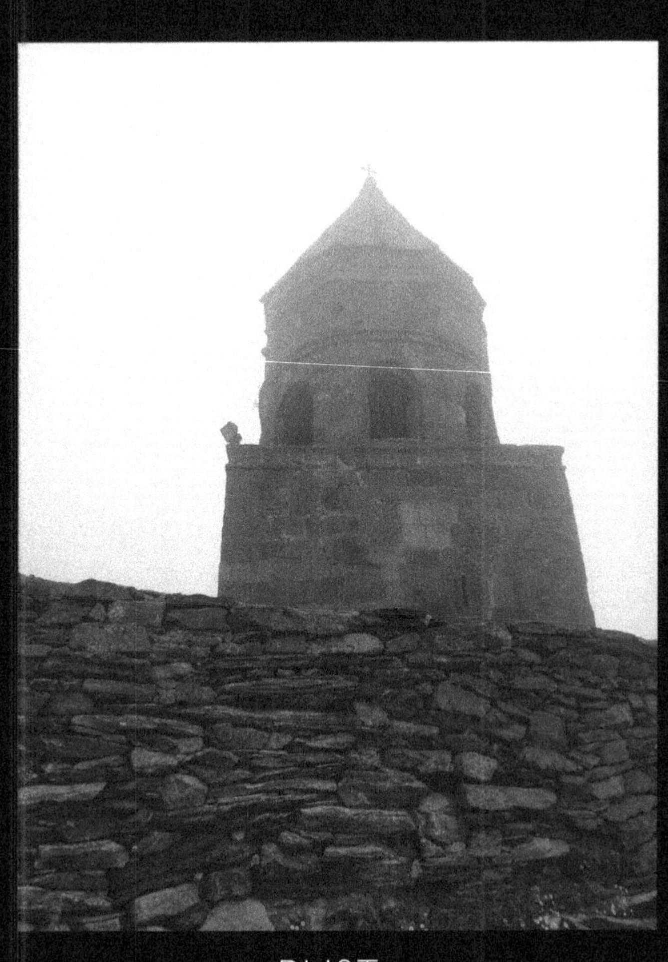

RUST

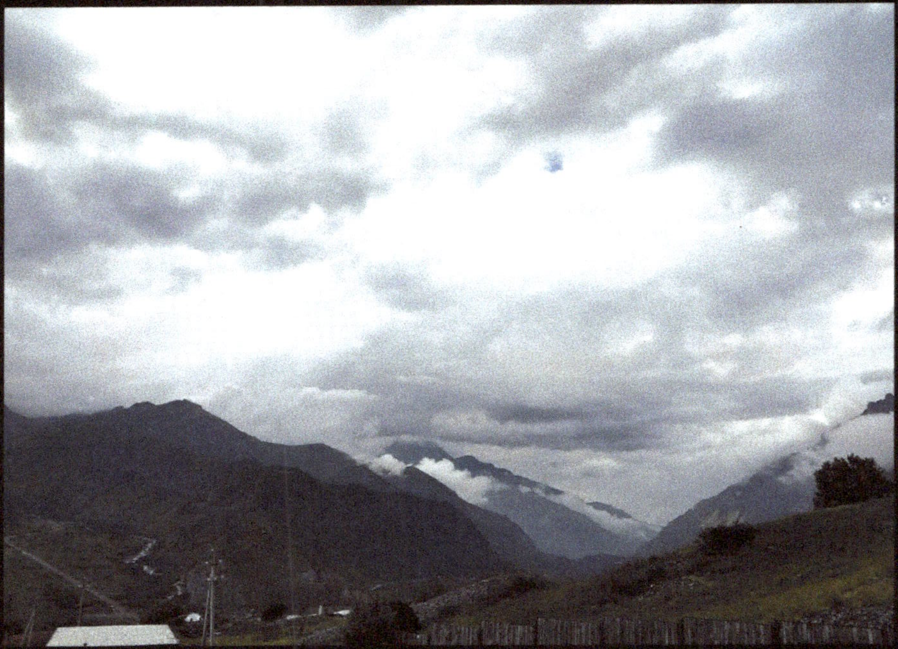

UNSHORN

About the Author

Laine Cunningham's books take readers around the world. *The Family Made of Dust* is set in the Australian Outback, while *Reparation* is a novel of the American Great Plains. Her women's travel adventure memoir *Woman Alone: A Six-Month Journey Through the Australian Outback* appeals to fans of *Wild* and *Eat Pray Love*.

Fiction

The Family Made of Dust

Beloved

Reparation

Nonfiction

Woman Alone

On the Wallaby Track: Australian Words and Phrases

Seven Sisters: Messages from Aboriginal Australia

Writing While Female or Black or Gay

The Zen of Travel
The Zen of Gardening
Zen in the Stable
The Zen of Chocolate
The Zen of Dogs

The Wisdom of Puppies
The Wisdom of Babies
The Wisdom of Weddings

Bikes of Berlin
Necropolises of New Orleans I & II
Ruins of Rome I & II
Ancients of Assisi I & II
Panoramas of Portugal
Nuances of New York
Glimpses of Germany
Impressions of Italy
Altitudes of the Alps
Knights Through the Ages
Coast of California
Utopia of the Unicorn
Flourishes of France
Portraits of Paris
Grandeur in the Republic of Georgia
Tableaus of Tbilisi